Malta & Gozo

An Artist's View
Richard Cole

For Richard
Happy BBC Days.
Richard Cole

Published in Malta by Miller Distributors Ltd
Miller House, Airport Way, Ħal Tarxien Road,
Luqua LQA 1814, Malta.
Tel: (+356) 21 66 44 88
E-mail: info@millermalta.com
Website: www.millermalta.com
              www.agendamalta.com

Copyright publication: Richard Cole
Copyright Illustrations & text: Richard Cole
Designer: Robin Cannon
Editor: Alan Giddings
Printed by: Gutenberg Press Ltd.
Published by: Miller Publications, section from Miller
                                 Distributors Ltd.

ISBN: 978 999 577 4554 (Paperback)
ISBN: 978 999 577 4639 (Hardback)

Sculpture in Freedom Square of the Grand Master Jean Parisot de la Valette by Joseph Chetcuti.

back in niches. These were erected by order of the Knights of Malta, who stipulated that every corner of the city should have a statue or monument. The stone buildings have wooden decorative panelled balconies supported by stone corbels that extend pleasingly over the streets. Many times I found myself instinctively drawn back to the busy harbour, watching the boats coming and going, many of which I noted were Chinese.

The main thoroughfare, Republic Street, is wide and leads you in a direct line through the main shopping centre all the way to the sea at Fort Elmo. In fact, all the roads are straight, built on a traditional grid system, and they all lead you to the sea that surrounds the rocky peninsula on three sides. I found that whilst exploring the city you have to be prepared to climb many flights of wide steps, but the view at the summit is always worth it. Especially impressive is the panorama from the Saluting Battery with the old cannons pointing across the Grand Harbour towards the three cities, Vittoriosa, Senglea and Kalkara.

San Gwann Street, Valletta.

VALLETTA

Valletta is an outstanding example of a walled city, built on a small peninsula of south - east Malta and full of baroque masterpieces. It occupies a key strategic position in the central Mediterranean that means it has been fought over for centuries. Its history reflects these competing conflicts and has defined how it is today with a wonderful collection of churches, palaces and monuments for the visiting tourist to admire.

The city of Valletta derives its name from Jean Parisot de Valette, the 49th Grand Master of the Order of Malta who planned the buildings and laid the first foundation stone in 1566. Various versions of his surname were in use, but one of the styles – de la Vallette – led to the city he founded being called Valletta.

Jean de Valette gained great military prestige when in 1565 he repulsed the superior Turkish invaders during the Great Siege of Malta but sadly died two years later and never saw the city's completion. He had engaged Francesco Laperelli to be the architect, who developed a grid system for the city without specific elite areas. Valletta was built as a fortress to defend its two harbours, but it expanded in concept to include large cathedrals and rich knights' palaces. Following his death, the new rulers of Malta, the Order of the Knights of St

John, commissioned Laperelli's assistant - the architect and military engineer of Sicilian origins Gerolamo Cassar - to continue his work and Cassar was responsible for overseeing a majority of the buildings. These include St John's Co - Cathedral, The Grandmaster's Palace and the Auberges. Valletta's architecture is mainly baroque in style and in 1980 it was granted the distinction of becoming a UNESCO World Heritage Site. A statue of Jean Parisot de Valette surveying his legacy now stands in Freedom Square.

Valletta was described in the 19th century as being one of the best fortified cities in the world and today the fortifications are still impressive, with bastions and curtain walls protecting the peninsular. Originally there were three gates to the city but now only two remain, City Gate and Victoria Gate.

When I first arrived in 1975, City Gate was the fourth incarnation to have stood on the site. It was designed in 1964 by Alziro Bergonzo in a 'Futurist Italian style'. There was a large opening in the centre to allow traffic to enter and two smaller ones on each side. As with most new buildings, it was highly criticised and controversial and the Chamber of Architects described it as being 'an architectural flop'.

Church of Notre Dame de Liesse.

The Fifth Gate designed by Renzo Piano.

of the French army two years later. The Victoria Gate now also displays coat of arms of Malta and Valletta carved in Maltese limestone.

Britain surrendered its rule of Malta in 1964 and it became a republic in 1974 under Prime Minister Dom Mintoff. It is thanks to the Mintoff cartoon I drew in *The Times* in 1975 that I made my first trip to Malta which inspired my love of the island. For British patriots there are still many nostalgic reminders on the island, primarily the telephone and post boxes. An indication of independence was that the various British coats of arms usually found on post boxes have been removed.

The fifth Gate is not so much to my way of thinking a Gate, more a passageway between two large blocks of stone with high blades of steel pointing skywards. It was an entirely new experience entering this recently designed quarter that has greatly changed since my last visit in 2009.

I must say that I agree with them, and fortunately in 2011 it was demolished to make way for the fifth Gate.

Victoria Gate was built by the British in 1885, designed by a Maltese architect Emanuele Luigi Galizia. It too replaced a gate, but it had the addition of a drawbridge over an excavated ditch. The gate is very flamboyant and celebratory

of British rule and you can still see the emblazoned lion and unicorn from the Royal coat of arms, acknowledging the British intervention after the Napoleonic invasion in 1798. At the request of the beleaguered Maltese, the British fleet blockaded the harbour with the additional help of Neapolitan and Portuguese forces and the siege that followed forced the the surrender

11

was an attractive iconic building built in 1866 by the English architect Edward Middleton Barry, who famously designed the Covent Garden Theatre in London.

After the war, the German prisoners (perhaps out of a shared associated guilt) offered to re - build it. Sadly not one mason was found among their ranks, so the offer was declined.

It was no surprise to learn that the whole refurbishment of the theatre and its environment was controversial. Eventually after lengthy discussions it was finally decided to build a modern theatre on the footprint of the bombed structure. Apparently the old ticket office had survived among the ruins and was able to be modernised and re - used. It was also agreed not to cover the new building with a roof but to leave it open to the elements. One evening I walked around the outside of the theatre during an operatic performance and the whole surrounding area was ringing to its tunes. It was an interesting experience and I look forward to eventually buying a ticket. The marriage of the old with the new is dramatic, exciting and brilliantly executed, and I don't mind if my personal appraisal is also controversial.

The whole area has been re - designed and rebuilt by the renowned Italian architect Renzo Piano. Two long, broad flights of stone steps dramatically soar up to another level on each side of the Gate; one is flanked by traditional wooden balconies and the other by the modern Parliament building. A large number of old buildings have had to be demolished in order to make way for this substantial redevelopment.

Further on is the newly built open - air theatre Pjazza Teatru Rjal with its ancient tall columns. It is sited on the remains of the old Valletta Opera House, which had survived an earlier fire disaster, but was finally destroyed by a direct bomb hit in 1942 during the Second World War. Originally it

View Of Fort St Angelo.

THE KAROZZIN DRIVERS

The *karozzin* drivers were parked in Bastion Square with their colourful, horse - drawn taxis, chatting together while they waited for a fare. They seemed to be an affable group of men so I asked if they would allow me to draw a few of their portraits. One of the cab drivers charged me a few coins to pose, but his fellow driver thought it was rather inhospitable and offered his services for free, a friendly gesture. He was pleased with the resulting drawing so we were both happy.

The *karozzin* carriages have been used since the mid - 19th century and were popular forms of transport during the days of the British Empire among visiting British soldiers and sailors. Their destinations were usually the shops or more commonly the bars and brothels nicknamed 'The Gut' in Strait Street. Times have moved on since then and the horse - drawn cabs are mainly used for tourists sight - seeing around Valletta, Mdina and Victoria or hired out for weddings. The journeys are normally accompanied by a colourful commentary from the driver, which I am told, can be very entertaining but not always historically accurate. The *karozzins* are often passed

George West, Mesida.

down through generations and great pride is taken with their appearance. I should like to think that the horses are also well looked after and given plenty of food and water whilst waiting for a fare, especially in the intense heat of the summer. It must be a tough life for the animals.

THE VINTAGE BUSES

The common way to get around the islands in 1975 was using the local buses, a travelling experience not to be missed. I can only describe them as single - decker boneshakers, their suspensions having long since given up because of the rough road surfaces. Despite their faults, though, they had great character reflecting the style of their owners, and provided an eventful ride. Many had religious shrines installed in glass cases behind the drivers facing the passengers, often quoting religious homilies and a salute to 'Good Queen Bess'. Hopefully they provided reassurance for a safe arrival for all the travellers.

When I returned in 2009, the old buses were still in service and I was able to remind myself of their delights and complete a few shaky sketches as we rumbled along the roads. But sadly on 3rd July 2011, all the vintage buses were phased out and a new company called *Arriva Malta* was formed that used modern vehicles.

The old buses may have been air polluters, unreliable, uneconomic and uncomfortable to ride in, but they did have a lot of character and will be missed, especially by their owner - drivers who customised and decorated them. The tradition of owner - drivers goes right back to 1905 when buses were first imported into Malta. At the end of the Second World War, some Maltese entrepreneurs bought old British army ambulances for conversion. Handmade bus bodies were welded onto the chassis in local workshops and decorated with American - type shiny chrome grills and

hubcaps, badges, large elaborate headlamps and personal decorations. The insides of the buses were also personalised with religious shrines, texts, lucky images and souvenirs. In those days anyone could become an owner - driver once they had obtained a licence and a vehicle. The buses were often parked outside their homes and became family heirlooms for their sons to inherit. The tradition after 1995 was that they should be painted in two colours separated by a horizontal red band under the windows, canary - yellow below and white above. Previously in the 80s they were green, and prior to that, they were colour coded according to the route they followed. The Gozo buses were more conservative, being all grey with a red band below the window.

A few renovated vintage buses can now be seen in an industrial heritage museum, whilst others can be hired for weddings and special occasions. I for one will miss them.

The colour has now drained out of the buses. In 2014, *Malta Public Transport* took over from *Arriva Malta* and painted all their buses white with a touch of green.

Interior of a vintage bus.

THE VALLETTA BUS TERMINUS

Drawing the Triton Fountain turned out to be tricky for me as it was situated on the roundabout for the buses going to their terminus in City Gate square, and I had to keep moving to avoid being run over. The terminus was very busy with buses arriving and departing, carrying hordes of tourists. Now the buses have been re - routed, and the area has become a pedestrian plaza that would have made drawing easier.

The Triton Fountain was designed by the Maltese sculptor Vincent Apap, and shows the Tritons holding up the basin, flexing their muscles in a self - conscious macho way. When I was there, the water wasn't cascading over everything so I was able to study the statues clearly.

THE GRAND MASTER'S PALACE

At the end of Republic Street and facing the Palazzo is The Grand Master's Palace which houses the Office of the President of Malta, the Palace State Rooms and the Armoury Museum. It was built by the Grand Master of the Order of St John between the 16th and 18th centuries.

The main gate leads into a courtyard which has a statue of the god Neptune centre stage, surrounded by exotic palm trees. The statue was commissioned by the Grand Master Alof de Wignacourt himself and rumour has it that it bears a strong resemblance to the man, but others believe that it was an Admiral Andrea Doria who agreed to pose naked for the statue. Either way, whoever lays claim to it must have had a great ego.

The Palace houses the Armoury Museum of the Order of St John and has a splendid collection containing over 500 items, mainly from two of the Grand Masters, La Valette and Alof de Wignacourt. The arsenal was originally installed in the Palace in 1604 and had enough arms and armour to equip an army of 1,000 soldiers, but during France's two - year occupation in 1798 - 1800, Napoleon stole a large portion of the collection following his policy of 'organised robbery of art treasures and

historic items.' Sadly during this period Malta was stripped of countless treasures. The present collection, presumably containing arms that escaped Napoleon's hands, was opened as a museum in 1860. Apparently with the death of a knight, his armoury automatically becomes the property of the Order and therefore cunningly enlarges the overall stock.

The collection boasts a large number of fierce weapons, firearms and cannons, and there is a particularly impressive

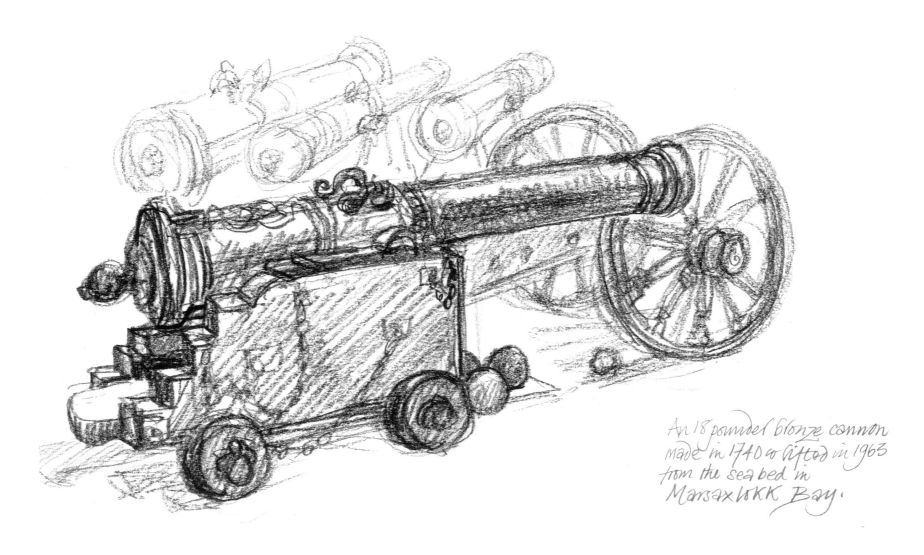

An 18 pounder bronze cannon made in 1740 or lifted in 1963 from the sea bed in Marsaxlokk Bay.

Dimech published 462 editions of his magazine, two novels, books of poetry and foreign language books. He gained followers from all classes keen for change, but suffered much hardship and oppression. Support from the Royal Shipyard dockworkers resulted in the British viewing him as a threat to their important Mediterranean base. The powerful Catholic Church also attacked him and he was eventually excommunicated. During the years 1911 - 12 they pitilessly persecuted him and his family, but he stood firm against powerful odds and the church finally conceded defeat and called a truce.

The First World War was the beginning of his final downfall as he was again arrested on false charges and accused of being a German spy. The British Governor of Malta deported him to Sicily and then to Egypt. He was arrested as a prisoner of war and ended up in a concentration camp in Alexandria until 1921. Winston Churchill, then Secretary of State for the Colonies, refused to release him. He suffered seven miserable years in prison and his health greatly deteriorated, and he died forlorn and alone on 17th April 1921. He was buried in an unmarked grave in Alexandria in Egypt.

After his death, faithful followers of Dimech continued his struggle but they too were treated harshly by the colonial government and publically disgraced. For many years Manwel Dimech was forgotten. His legacy, however, lives on and has been finally recognised.

Franciscan Father Tony Briffa of the Church of St Mary of Jesus & parishioner.

THE CHURCH OF ST PAUL'S SHIPWRECK

Unlike many churches in Valletta with their grand entrances to encourage congregations to enter, the approach to the Church of St Paul's Shipwreck is more discreet with its doors opening from a flight of steps off a narrow street. I was invited to enter into a large anteroom where an attendant was trying to persuade female tourists to cover their heads with scarves conveniently provided. He wasn't having much success as the women either ignored him or were unaware of this respectful convention.

I was astonished as I entered the church by its sheer size and the elaborate decoration of its interior. Paintings, sculptures and murals of religious subjects surrounded me on all sides, and the feeling was one of opulence. I was staggered that so many artworks had been collected together and lavishly displayed over what seemed every available surface. The floor was covered in marble tombstones beautifully decorated with inlaid stones depicting skulls and heraldic family crests.

Commemorating St Paul, who was shipwrecked on the island in 60 AD, the church holds a few religious remnants supposedly associated with him, namely his wrist bone and a fragment from the stone on which he was beheaded, gifted to the church by Pope Pius V111.

On my way out I noticed a sign that directed me down into a crypt of a revered cleric. It was refreshingly simple and relatively unadorned.

THE FEAST OF ST PETER AND ST PAUL

I arrived in Valletta at the end of June to discover to my delight that the main thoroughfare was lined with richly coloured confraternity banners of orange and red draped along the streets or stretched across them from one side to the other. They continued on most of the streets towards the harbour and around the church of St Paul's Shipwreck, which was the clue to the oncoming celebrations. The Feast of St Peter and St Paul was imminent and would last for three days, apparently commemorating the beheading of St Paul. There is an even larger Feast in February around the Cathedral of St John that commemorates the shipwrecking of St Paul on the island of Malta in 60 AD. His arrival brought Christianity to Malta.

The first two days prior to the major events involve church services, an evening procession with the statue of St Peter and an excellent street recital by the marching band. The Maltese do appreciate a religious festival and they turned up in big numbers to witness the main procession that travels through the streets from the church to the Siege Bell Memorial in the harbour.

The statue of St. Paul had been removed from its glass - fronted cubicle in the church and placed in the street surrounded by its white robed bearers. The edifice of St Paul was sculpted by Melchior Gafà in 1656. It has a very dramatic bearing, with his right arm stretching forward in a triumphant gesture, his left holding a large religious tome and two cherubs sitting at his feet.

I have always been very interested in the iconography of religious carvings as my father was an ecclesiastical wood carver and I grew up admiring his skilled craftsmanship. To my

knowledge he carved many crucifixes and religious saints, cherubs and angels playing musical instruments, but I only saw them in their natural wooden state. I knew that some of them would end up being painted and gilded like Gafà's. The majority of the sculptures in the churches are made of plaster or papier mâché, but the wooden sculptures have to be carefully preserved and looked after to protect them from warping and cracking due to the extremes of temperature and humidity. A recent procession in Valletta with the Gafà statue had to be cancelled to prevent damage because it unfortunately rained heavily.

A team of white robed bearers carried another sculpture, this time representing the severed head of St Paul. It is cast in solid silver and placed on a small section of a stone column that is claimed to be the one on which he was beheaded. In addition, a devoted follower carried a bejewelled silver sculpture of a muscular forearm that purports to contain a most treasured religious relic of St Paul, a portion of his right wrist bone. At the base a gold sculptured snake curls around the arm, symbolic of the venomous bite St Paul miraculously survived after he was shipwrecked on the island.

The procession was assembled with the marching band to the rear. The religious participants assembled were priests, canons and friars in their

colourful regalia, altar boys, cross and lantern bearers and a mace bearer in a bright red robe. There was a roll of drums, the band struck up, and the procession moved off with the statue of St Paul being rocked gently from side to side as the bearers took the full weight. When the band had finished playing a tune the procession came to a halt. It allowed the bearers carrying the heavy sculptures to place them on supports in order to rest or change personnel. There was no hurry, and there was plenty of time to chat and enjoy the atmosphere. A display of fireworks crackled over the harbour and at times the music of the band was accompanied by an enthusiastic cheering crowd as confetti drifted down over the procession from the overhead apartment windows. I was amused to find that in addition to shredded paper, the confetti was made up from old torn up lotto tickets.

The lengthy procession finally reached the Siege Bell Memorial, which was built to

commemorate the 50th anniversary of the presentation of the George Cross to the island. The sun was setting and an address was delivered from the steps by members of the clergy. As we walked back along the route, fireworks were still being let off and young children were enjoying themselves scooping up and playing with the confetti that had whitened the road.

Vincent Borg, the Archpriest of Saint Paul's Parish Church Valletta in discussion with his fellow priests during a musical interlude in the procession.

STRAIT STREET

I had heard a great deal about the reputation of Strait Street as the red light district of Valletta, nicknamed crudely by the visiting sailors and merchant seamen as 'The Gut'. It was a popular first stop among men in need of alcohol, female company and entertainment, right up until the 1970s, when the area went into a rapid decline. I was interested to find out what historic elements remained.

In a Catholic country like Malta, the quarter was considered shameful and only spoken about in hushed tones, but nobody could ignore the fact that it had become an important social hub creating employment in a part of the city that was very poor and neglected. Ignoring the vice, employment was to be found in the variety of bars, music halls and cabaret venues. There was a cosmopolitan clientele over the decades, with Italians, French, British and Americans all having an influence on the street's culture. As well as the attraction of women, music was an important element throughout the bars, and Americans mainly from the Sixth Fleet introduced jazz and popular music to the street. Female impersonators and cross - dressing performers were also among the popular acts.

Inevitably riotous behaviour and fights often broke out among visiting navies defending their 'nation's honour,' invariably fuelled by copious amounts of alcoholic drinks. On a more positive note, some successful international cabaret artists and singers cut their teeth in the music halls; a notable success from the 50s and 60s was easy - listening singer Frankie Vaughan, who was based in Malta during his National Service. His association

with Strait Street obviously didn't impede his career as he eventually became one of the most popular British performers, known as Mr Moonlight from one of his many hit records.

Malta's independence finally sounded the death knell of Strait Street as the British navy's visits declined and the bars and music venues slowly closed and were boarded up. Walking along the narrow street I was anxious to find remnants of some of the notorious establishments with such redolent names as Silver Force, Blue Peter Bar, Egyptian Queen, White Star and Smiling Prince Bar. I had previously read a book by the Maltese author George Cini called Strada Stretta that vividly brought the street to life with its interviews from people who lived and worked there. Their recollections were so vivid that I imagined as I moved from one door to another I could hear the music and the babble of different languages emanating from the ancient walls. A photograph of the bar signs from the era showed that the Smiling Prince Bar was number 124, and the Blue Peter Bar was number 96, but gradually the traces of the street's previous activities are being eliminated.

The street is now in the process of being gentrified with lawyers' offices, shops and restaurants occupying the old premises. One such British retail establishment, Marks and Spencer, now occupies two premises that face one another on opposite sides of the street. It is rumoured that conscious of the streets notoriety and not wishing to have their own reputation tainted by association, they decided to connect the two shops by a covered bridge that spans the street. The sanctification is complete.

THE TATTOOIST

The only visible business I found in the street that has survived from that bawdy era is the tattoo parlour at 87 Strait Street. It has been owned by three generations of the Psoile family and I was greeted by Renald Psoile, a middle - aged man of Italian origin who spoke very little English. I explained as best I could that I was not interested in having a tattoo, which initially disappointed him, but that I would very much like to do a drawing of him displaying his personal tattoos. He became enthusiastic and agreed to strip off to his waist. I have to admit that I have always been prejudiced against the modern trend in Britain towards having a tattoo, especially among young women. His tattoos, however, were to my mind tastefully designed with a strong Japanese influence and not excessive, with koi carp curling around his right shoulder and arm, swimming onto his chest. As I drew him, he explained that his grandfather Charlie Psiole started tattooing 80 years ago in the premises and passed the business onto his father Tony, and then to him and his two brothers, Wayne and Rode. I became aware

whilst I was drawing that there was an elderly lady standing behind me giving a running commentary in Italian on the progression of my drawing. Fortunately for me, when I had finally finished it there was an enthusiastic cry from both Renald and the onlooker of 'Bravissimo'.

Aparently the Catholic church disapproves of the practice of tattooing, considering it pagan and heretical, and in certain quarters it can make employment difficult. Renald told me that he has old clients who return to have their tattoos refreshed and brightened up, but this is declining with the introduction of modern inks.

I learnt from an English tattooist Guy Lee, who has a tattoo parlour in Mellieha and describes himself as 'a trained killer and ex - Royal Marine veteran', that he has some clients who have a new tattoo added to their collection when they are depressed. The pain endured during the tattooing can for some people apparently serve as a welcome release of tension and the continuous chat during the operation acts as a therapy.

Guy practises what he preaches and has some impressive tattoos on his body except for one particular area of his skin. He likes to train his apprentices in the art of tattooing and claims that the greatest thing you can do for your students is to offer them a part of your body to practise on. I felt this was a very generous and selfless offer, but what, I asked, happens if the tattoo is a total failure? Guy lifted up his left leg and showed me his ankle. He had completely blacked it out!

His wife, however, was a beautiful English rose untouched by his tattooing skills.

I was amused by the tattoos I saw whilst walking around Valletta that are on the backs of peoples arms and legs, obviously placed there for the appreciation or otherwise of a following onlooker and yet divorced from the view of the owner.

SAMMY MURGO JAZZ MUSICIAN

The Bridge Bar in Valletta is one of those delightful corners you find in a town that you stumble across joyfully. The Bar hosts a regular jazz session every Friday and when I went there, I watched and listened to Sammy Murgo and his quartet light up the place.

The Bar is wonderfully situated on the pedestrian bridge that leads down to the harbour and the enthusiastic audience enjoy the music at tables in front of the band stand or lounge on cushions on the stone steps. On a balmy summer night, there is no better place to hear the music and relax.

Chatting with the bar owner, I learned that Sammy Murgo was known as 'The Living Legend' because, at 81 years old, he was one of the old - timers who had originally earned his living playing in the bars in Strait Street in an era long gone. Having heard him perform, I was eager to draw him and ask him about his experiences so we arranged to meet the following week.

He told me about his life as a jazz musician. Born in 1936, he was encouraged by his musician father to take up the violin at seven years old and by the time he reached 13, he was playing in the local church alongside his father. Close by in Floriana, there was an area of bars and clubs known as The Gut, which is where Sammy started playing regularly at 14, keeping a low profile until he reached the legal age of 18. The experience was invaluable and his profile developed when he moved to Strait Street with its many bars and music halls, with legendary names like Lucky Wheel, Silver Horse, White Horse, Four Aces and Folies Bergère. Life was exciting.

Despite his musical success, there were always ups and downs, and he maintained some job security working for the post office. He earned a salary of £24 a month but playing in the bars he could earn £2 - £3 extra in tips a night, organised by girls that he referred to as hostesses. He recalls with a gleam in his eye that the 50s and 60s were exciting times to be working as a young man, 'The Good Happy Days' he called it. The Strait Street bars and clubs attracted British, American, Italian and Maltese sailors and soldiers and fights were not uncommon, an obvious hazard for any musician.

In the 50s Sammy was persuaded by the musician Paul Arnaud to change the violin for the saxophone. He bought an alto saxophone for £65 and never looked back, playing on occasions with visiting international artists including the British giant John Dankworth.

At 81, Sammy Murgo is still playing his heart out.

VICTORY DAY REGATTA

The exciting and spectacular regattas take place in Valletta's harbour twice a year on 31st March and 8th September, attracting thousands of spectators and supporters to the races. Both the dates are significant because they commemorate important historical dates for Malta. The first regatta in the calendar year is Freedom Day, celebrating the departure in 1979 of the British troops and the Royal Navy. The September regatta is Victory Day and celebrates a number of significant events: the end of the bloody Great Siege of Malta in 1565 by the Turkish Empire, the end of the French

Blockade in 1800, and the armistice in 1943 of Mussolini's fascist regime in Italy that ended the incessant heavy bombing of the Maltese islands. It is a lot to celebrate and the Maltese enter into the festivities with great enthusiasm.

Open - topped buses full of supporters arrive waving flags and cheering, then assembling themselves on the quays and the bastion walls on both sides of the harbour to get a good vantage point to watch the races. Many supporters wear their rowing club colours and cheer long and loud to encourage their crews as they approach the finishing line. The atmosphere is added to by the stirring music played by a group of musicians seated under a nearby canvas awning.

It's a spectacular style of rowing, with half of a boat crew standing while the other half are seated. It's very energetic and demonstrates a range of rowing skills including a keen sense of balance. The boats race down a course of 1,040 metres in a frenzied fashion with the cheers of their supporters ringing in their ears.

I watched the drama unfold from the harbour side of Valletta with the imposing backdrop of Fort St Angelo and the three cities of Cospicua, Birgu and Senglea.

54

the harbour. They then rowed up the estuary to the start of the races. The different rowing clubs can be recognised by the brightly coloured flags that are attached to the forestems of their racing craft.

Whilst drawing and studying the bastion wall and the buildings around the club's premises I noticed some of the damage which is still evident in the structure of the walls

The racing boats have been developed from the traditional rowing boats that used to ferry passengers across the harbour in a more sedate fashion. They have been modified and streamlined into racing boats and painted with the club colours, and now compete against each other to win the coveted Aggregrate Shield. The Maltese traditional boats have intriguing names, like frejgatini, dghajjestal - pass, tal - midalji and kajjikki, and the teams taking part are from towns around the islands, including Cospicua, Marsa, Birzebbuga, Vittoriosa, Marsamxett, Isla and Kalkara. There are ten races that are subdivided into two different categories and the spectacle lasts for most of the day.

There was a lot of preparation required by the competing clubs and I spent an interesting time watching the local club in Valletta carrying their racing boats from the boat house which was housed in the interior of the bastion and launching their craft down the slipway into

manager in the café where I was sheltering exclaimed excitedly 'I have been working in Valletta for five months and this is the first heavy rainfall we have had. Incredible!' The headlines of the Malta Independent declared the following morning that it was 'The End of Summer'. It was also the end of the reign of the Marsa rowing club that won the Aggregate Shield for the last three years as the coveted trophy for 2017 was now in the hands of the impressive Cospicua oarsmen.

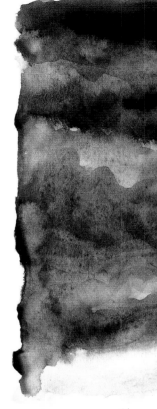

caused by the heavy bombing during the Second World War. It was a timely reminder of the suffering the Maltese have endured and the freedom that these races celebrate.

I very much enjoyed sketching the events but by lunchtime dark clouds had started forming over the harbour and eventually an enormous thunderstorm erupted. The thunder and lightning was so intense that it would have easily drowned out the loud fire - cracking explosions from the fireworks that are constantly let off over the harbour entrance on balmy summer evenings. The ensuing downpour was very heavy and the pavements were flooded in minutes. The

The Old Customs House.

NATIONAL WAR MUSEUM

The National War Museum housed in Fort St Elmo commemorates much of Malta's military history, particularly the two world wars.

Malta has been affected by invaders from many of its neighbours from its earliest days, from the Bronze Age around 2,500 BC, through occupation by the Romans, the Phoenicians, the Carthaginians, the Byzantines, the Arabs and the Normans up to the Middle Ages when the Knights of the Order of St John arrived in 1530. The Great Siege of Malta by the Ottomans followed in 1565; they were eventually repulsed and the aftermath saw the rebuilding and fortification of Valletta during the 17th and 18th centuries. The rule by the Knights finally ended when Napoleon's forces occupied the island from 1798 - 1800 only to be defeated by the British forces under Nelson aided and abetted by a Maltese population uprising.

Under British rule, Malta became a strategic Mediterranean naval base during the First and Second World Wars. Malta suffered enormous deprivation and destruction by heavy bombing during the Second World War with its resistence and heroism commemorated by the British nation awarding the Maltese population the George Cross, the highest civilian award for bravery in the face of the enemy.

The Museum is most proud of Roosevelt's Jeep 'Husky,' the George Cross and one of the three Gloster Sea Gladiator biplanes (number N5520) that bravely defended the island during the War. They were surprisingly the only fighting planes available and were known affectionately as 'Faith, Hope and

Charity'. 'Faith' is on display, but sadly it is without its wings which were lost when it was left derelict after the war.

There is a dramatic re - enactment of Operation Pedestal (Santa Marija Convoy) projected on the floor in one of the museum's rooms that I found quite compelling. The task of the Royal Navy was to protect the Merchant Navy convoy delivering vital supplies to a besieged Malta. Despite heavy bombardment by Mussolini's air force, submarine attacks and the loss of British cargo ships, aircraft carriers and battleships, the surviving convoy managed against enormous odds to relieve Malta, then on the brink of collapse. On 15th August 1942, the crippled oil tanker S.S. Ohio, holed below the waterline and sinking, was towed into Grand Harbour supported by two Royal Navy destroyers H.M.S. Ledbury and H.M.S. Penn strapped to its sides. They were greeted by a large and jubilant cheering crowd. Malta was saved for the moment and could now fight on.

General Eisenhower's personal Willys Jeep 'HUSKY' used by him before the invasion of Sicily in 1943.

SANTA MARIJA CHAPEL, BALZAN

One day I was exploring the quiet streets around my hotel in Balzan and discovered the delightful Chapel of Santa Marija. While I was sketching, I spotted a priest in his clerical robes followed by an altar boy swinging an incense censer working his way down the road visiting all the houses. I asked the local grocer what the priest was doing and was informed that it was the Festival of Blessing the Houses. The tradition was that the priest would visit the homes in his parish and in exchange for a blessing he would receive an unsolicited donation for the church.

A friend related a story of his own experience as an altar boy when he also followed his priest on a parishioner circuit. He remembers that after the blessing and incense were spread around the room, alcoholic drinks were then offered to the assembled parties. Not wishing to be impolite, he frequently accepted the kind offer. His career finally came to a dramatic end when he returned home late one night much the worse for wear to the surprise and annoyance of his parents.

61

IL MIRAKLU TAL-BOMBA
9TA APRIL, 1942

THE ROTUNDA OF MOSTA

When I arrived at the Rotunda of Mosta, a heavy storm was in progress and people were rushing around trying to find suitable shelter, especially inside the church. Obviously when painting and drawing interesting sites, good weather is usually better than bad, but in this case the stormy backdrop showed the Rotunda features in a dramatic and effective way.

I managed to find a suitable place out of the rain in a shop doorway and started sketching, as shafts of light cut through the black clouds scudding over the Rotunda's wet, shiny dome. Numerous coaches were picking up or dropping off tourists and umbrellas were being unfurled and opened up as people hurried for shelter towards the open doors. The umbrellas created the title of my painting, 'The Domes of Mosta.'

The neoclassical church was built between 1833 and 1865 on the site of a Renaissance church and purports to have the third largest unsupported dome in the world, which is truly impressive. With no central supporting pillars, the light descending from above fills the space inside spectacularly, and illuminates the geometric pattern of the interior of the dome.

You might be surprised to see a bomb on display in the sacristy, but there's a good reason for this. During the Second World War on 9th April 1942, the church and the congregation of 250 parishioners had a fortunate escape when two German Luftwaffe bombs dropped on it during a mass fortunately failed to explode. One pierced the roof and bounced off the walls while the other landed outside in the square. The bombs were defused and a replica one displayed as a reminder of a small miracle.

The Road to Mdina

MDINA

My visit to the ancient medieval city of Mdina enabled me to use the modern bus fleet for the first time since my last visit in 2009. I was intrigued to see if the new buses had adopted the religious shrine situated behind the driver so characteristic of the old boneshakers, but I was disappointed. All I found was a sticker claiming that 'Jesus Saves', a pale reminder. However, at least the bus journey from the terminus in Valletta was smoother than before as the modern suspension was able to cope with some of the rougher roads. We sped on alongside the stony fields edged with prickly pears and on the distant horizon the domed red roof of Mdina Cathedral came into view. I got off the bus in Rabat and walked through the gardens.

Mdina is somewhat of a medieval classic, a fortified, walled city built by the Phoenicians around 700 BC on one of the highest points of the island. It was known as the Silent City, and acted as the seat of the municipal government in Malta up until the middle of the 16th century when it was supplanted by Valletta.

Outside in front of the entrance to the Citadel I discovered a terminus not for buses, but for the karozzin drivers and their horse - drawn carriages. Business was brisk and noisy, conducted in a variety of languages. Eager tourists queued in a line to be driven in style around the sights.

The city is entered via a narrow stone bridge with a dry moat below and high walls above that enclose the magnificent 14th and 15th century palaces. These are the

Gateway to Mdina

residences of some of the oldest Maltese aristocratic families and are something of a medieval time warp.

Mdina has a population of just 300 and no cars other than those owned by the citizens are permitted within the city walls, with the exception of hearses, wedding cars and emergency vehicles. Nevertheless, with the influx of the tourist trade life has become noisier. I could hear the regular clip clop of the karozzin carriage horses echoing around the city as the drivers gave their passengers a potted history of the historic sights.

The tall buildings create natural cooling air currents and walking around the narrow streets is very enjoyable as you discover at first hand a rich architectural heritage, a fascinating mix of the medieval and the baroque.

The Palazzo Falson Historic House Museum is one such gem. The second oldest building in the city dating back to the 13th century and named after its original owner, it is now run under the management of Fondazzjoni Patrimonju Malti who have restored the building and the contents to their former glory. The last occupant of the Palazzo was an eccentric Swedish gentleman Capt. Olof Frederick Gollcher OBE (1889 - 1962) who was an artist, a passionate collector of objects and a philanthropist.

He had a wide range of interests and, with the advantage of being very rich, he was able to build up a diverse collection of treasures in his home. His fortune, incidentally, was inherited from his father's shipping

Courtyard of Palazzo Falson

dial shows ten numbers, the day being divided into 10 hours, and the hours are divided into 100 minutes and 100 seconds. The decimal idea eventually ran out of favour and was abandoned in 1806.

Closer to home is a delightful pen and ink watercolour landscape painting by the artist and poet Edward Lear (1889 - 1962), an Englishman better known for his nonsense limericks and verse who visited Malta on many occasions.

The most bizarre artefact was in the armoury - a metal chastity belt which was quite gruesome in appearance and must have caused the unfortunate wearer great discomfort. It was apparently used in medieval times to protect a woman's chastity while her husband was away fighting, but it is now generally thought to be a mythical Victorian invention. It was a favourite party piece of Olof Gollcher who had great delight in showing it to his visitors. Gollcher was a promising artist

company – the Gollcher Group - that still operates in Malta.

I was fortunate to be given a tour around the museum by its enthusiastic curator, Francesca Balzan. We started in the beautiful courtyard that was bathed in sun and had blazing red bougainvillea flowers cascading down from the balcony, and then proceeded to move from one fascinating room heaving with treasures to another. These included amongst others, an armoury, a library of ancient books, maps, paintings, clocks, silver, sailing memorabilia, oriental carpets, antique furniture and marine archaeology. Viewing the treasured collection of Olof Gollcher in what was once his home gave the museum an unusual but intimate appeal.

The most valuable item in the collection is a fob watch made by a favourite watchmaker of King Louis XV1, Robert Robin (1742 - 1799), made in Paris in 1797 and signed Robin à Paris No.2. Only three were ever made. It is a fascinating clock because it uses 'French Revolutionary Time' which is decimal. The watch

himself, and one room contains a selection of his paintings, studio furniture and art materials plus some impressive early prints he made when he lived in Rome.

The building that towers above the city is the baroque Cathedral of St Paul, built on the site where the apostle, after being shipwrecked on the island, was said to have met with the Roman Governor Publius. The original cathedral was almost totally destroyed in 1693 by a violent Sicilian earthquake leaving only the sacristy and the choir standing. Luckily the Maltese architect Lorenzo Gafà had strengthened the structure of the building twelve years earlier that prevented total destruction. Fortunately some important artworks by the artist Mattia Preti also survived the earthquake including a painting on the altarpiece depicting St Paul's conversion and a fresco of his shipwreck. The marble baptismal font and the beautifully carved

Irish oak sacristy door also survived and are incorporated into the new Cathedral.

Fortuitously Lorenzo Gafà was well prepared for such an eventuality, as he had been working on a design for a new baroque style cathedral. Eight months prior to the earthquake, he had built a wooden model of his design and submitted the plans for approval, and they had been accepted. The site had been almost cleared by the seismic tremors so he was immediately commissioned to re - build the Cathedral which was completed by 1702 in just nine years. The dome of the Cathedral is a striking architectural feat engineered by Gafà and can be seen for miles around as it dominates the skyline. The two spires each contain six bells that can be clearly heard across the surrounding countryside.

The Cathedral has a museum in Archbishop's Square that was originally a diocesan seminary. The entrance façade is elaborately decorated and two naked male figures with arms up - stretched support the balcony on their heads. The museum houses religious items, paintings and archives as you would expect, but I was delighted to find that they also have an excellent collection of the German Renaissance artist Albrecht Dürer's woodcuts, lithographs and copperplate engravings, together with some fine Goya prints. The 11th century illuminated hymnals are beautiful and also worthy of close inspection.

The square was teeming with tourists as I left the Citadel and the karrozzin horse drawn carriages were weaving their way through the pedestrians.

As I exited by the main gate I noticed the entrance to the

Mdina dungeons that apparently contain quite scary, realistic models of medieval torture and executions. Aparently not recommended for children, nor me I decided.

NATURAL HISTORY MUSEUM

The Natural History Museum is on the right as you enter through the main gate in the Palazzo de Vilhena. Grand marble staircases lead you up to the exhibition rooms on three floors. The museum has a geology and fossil collection that explains Malta's landscape together with a display case of reptiles found on the islands, including four different snakes, a chameleon, lizards and a turtle. Particularly impressive is a giant lobster found in local waters which is one metre in length.

The Museum also has a collection of the birds recorded in the islands and is at pains to mention that they are against the killing of birds and other wildlife, and that the majority of the specimens have been part of the collection for several decades. This is mainly because shooting of birds in Malta is a very controversial subject. In fact, following a referendum in 2015 to continue this activity, Malta is the only EU country that allows recreational spring hunting and migratory birds are most at risk on their annual routes across the islands. I was very interested to see which birds are protected and which are considered fair game. Some very scarce visitors like the redwing, fieldfare, mistle thrush and grey plover are not protected. The ring ousel, reed and corn bunting together with all the raptors are

protected, but it must be almost impossible to police with so many trigger - happy hunters around. There are 10,000 legally licenced hunters in Malta and they are allowed to shoot 100,000 turtle doves each season on their migratory course.

Spain shoots just 8,000. Curiously, the blue rock thrush made its way onto a famous LMI coin, the equivalent of the wren on the British old farthing coin.

THE RABAT CATACOMBS

A visit to the catacombs in Rabat gives you a choice of three sites. If you approach from visiting the Citadel, the first one you reach is the small picturesque baroque Church of St Cataldus dedicated to an Irish Bishop. It was built in 1745 over a medieval crypt that was in turn built over a Christian hypogeum. The church is less commercial than the other venues and invites you to explore its hypogeum with a voluntary donation. The experience gives you a flavour in miniature of what you can expect to see at the other extensive and more expensive venues.

The second site is St Paul's Catacombs which is a very large labyrinth covering an area of 2,000 square metres of underground galleries and tombs built between the fourth and ninth centuries, but you are only permitted to access 24 of them, each through a separate entrance. It is like descending into a burrow and then returning to daylight. The catacombs were carved out in medieval times in the soft globigerina limestone using animal horns and flints, the only tools then available. The mining conditions must have been horrendous with the stone dust and the darkness illuminated only by oil lamps and flaming torches.

The bodies of the dead were then placed in the tombs and the babies in carved out niches.

The skeletons have been removed long ago and a few specimens can be viewed in the National Museum. The funeral ceremonies

St Cataldus Church.

appear to have been inter - denominational as carved symbols suggest that Christian, Jewish and Pagan burials were placed alongside one another.

The third catacomb open to the public is the Catacomb of St Agatha who was tortured and killed for her faith in 251 AD and died a martyr. One enters a crypt that was enlarged in the Middle Ages and is decorated with frescoes of saints painted in 1200 AD and 1480 AD. Sadly they are in a very poor state of preservation but are nevertheless fascinating to see. Finally after negotiating low narrow passageways one reaches what is thought to be Malta's oldest rock - carved church. The visit here was accompanied by an informative tour guide who I found to be a great help in understanding the site.

The St Cataldus Catacomb showing the 'Agape Table' used for Commemoration Meals of the dead relatives.

73

PASTIZZI

A pastizzi is a popular snack commonly sold in small take - away shops that bake them on the premises but you can also find them in bars and cafés. Originally an Arabic food, it is made with flaky filo pastry and filled with mainly mushy peas and onions, sometimes flavoured with anchovies or with ricotta cheese and parsley. They are best eaten hot straight from the oven when the pastry is crisp. They require a certain eating technique, however, as the pastry flies in all directions if you are not careful. I find them delicious and a very cheap filling lunchtime snack. They sell for around 30 centimes each, so two plus a glass of tea at my favourite pastizzi café in Rabat, Crystal Palace, costs only one euro and 10 cents. Amazing value! The tea

is served in a glass, poured from a teapot in the old fashioned way and topped up with hot water from a kettle; it tastes pretty good. Very nostalgic memories for me of the greasy spoon roadside cafés I grew up with in London.

Our Lady Of Mount Carmel

I was travelling back on the bus from Marsaskala to Valletta having spent the morning drawing the harbour and the fishing boats. I spent my time observing the buildings we passed which were generally fairly pedestrian and unremarkable, when suddenly a gap appeared in a line of shops. I caught the glimpse out of the corner of my eye of a stunning piece of architecture set back from the road. Not baroque, but a modern designed church.

I was so surprised that I immediately got off at the next bus stop and walked back to seek out this modern edifice. I had no idea where I was but was told by a passerby that I was in Fgura and the church was Roman Catholic, run by the Carmelite Fathers and named after Our Lady of Mount Carmel. The apex of the façade was stunning, with a cross and a hanging bronze sculpture of Jesus suspended in front. A strip of stained glass on either side of the church dramatically rises up from its base.

The church was designed by architect and engineer Godfrey Azzopardi and was built in 1988. Its structural support is made from reinforced concrete. Architect Edward Micallef, described the church in 'The Architect', *'The layout from the exterior is pyramidical, with a triangular opening on each four sides, which gives the impression of a floating building aimed to appear as a tent'*.

I was determined to see the famous Hypogeum in Paola even though it can be tricky to get a ticket at the height of the visitor season and on this visit to Malta my time was limited. This remarkable underground burial site was used between 4,000 and 2,500 BC and to protect the chambers from deterioration, only a small number of visitors are allowed to enter each day. However, a few tickets are held back at a premium price for viewing on the following day and as all the normal tickets were sold out in advance for the next three months, my options were limited. Just twelve tickets were available for sale at 9am at the National War Museum ticket office and even though I was early, I was fourth when I joined the queue. Despite the first person in the queue requesting five of the twelve tickets available, it turned out that it was to be my lucky day as I was offered the last ticket for the next day's noon visit.

After all this palaver, I wanted to ensure that no time was wasted and so I arrived early at Paola the next day. As I wandered around the area, I realised that I was close to the Tarxien Temples and so went for a look. This hugely important prehistoric site is in the centre of the residential quarter of Tarxien and was declared to be a UNESCO world heritage site in 1992, along with other megalithic temples.

The three Neolithic and Bronze Age Temples were a chance discovery in 1913 by local farmer Lorenzo Despott. It is a vast site stretching throughout Tarxien and contains some rare and unusual carvings, particularly of domestic animals. The original decorated altar, spiral carvings and the remains of a large female statue are now kept in the National Museum of

Archaeology and replicas have been placed on site so it is possible to see how everything fitted together. I visited the Museum to get the finer details for my drawings.

Metal walkways have been inserted into the temples to allow visitors a proper pathway through the stone edifices and constructions. Whilst I was drawing, inquisitive visitors' heads would occasionally pop up over and around the stones to find their bearings as though they were in a large maze. Similar to the Temples of Hagar Quim and Mnajdra, a large canopy covered the stones for added protection from the elements.

And so I finally made it to the Hypogeum. The visit started with an informative, explanatory short film that gave an historical background to the site and before we embarked on our underground tour, we had to deposit cameras, bags and in my case sketchbooks and drawing materials in designated lockers. It was a disappointment not to be able to record my visit graphically but on reflection, it would have been impractical as the passages are narrow and cramped and the ceilings very low. The entrances to the chambers are beautifully carved with elegant proportions unlike the Rabat catacombs.

The site was apparently discovered by chance when a resident decided to carve out a reservoir in the limestone underneath their house and accidentally broke through into a burial chamber. It is estimated that some 7,000 bodies were interred in the Hypogeum.

The visit was very memorable and certainly worth all the tense queuing involved in buying a ticket.

Tarxien Temple's decorated altar and relief sculptures at the National Museum of Archaeology, Valletta.

This colossal statue with
pleated skirt would have
originally stood at
nearly 3 metres.

1924

MARSAXLOKK

I visited Marsaxlokk harbour midweek
as I was told that the fish market and the
restaurants on a Sunday attract hordes of
visiting tourists, especially during the

summer months. It turned out to be very good advice as the harbour was relatively quiet and I was able to move around easily, finding some good places from which to draw. While I worked, the brightly coloured boats of Malta's largest fishing fleet were gently rocking in the harbour and the fishermen were occupied with ship maintenance, mending their nets and scraping off paintwork from the hulls. The traditional Maltese 'Luzzu' fishing boats are based on a design derived from the ancient Phoenician fishing vessels and are painted in the traditional bright colours. Carved symbols of the 'Eyes of Osiris' are attached to their prows as it is believed that they will warn off evil spirits.

The view from the harbourside is dominated by the Church of our Lady of Pompeii. This Roman Catholic church has hedged its bets believing that in addition to its religious doctrine, it has another unusual way of fighting off evil spirits. There are two clocks on the church, one regularly showing the proper time, but the other is a painted mural showing the clock's hands set a few minutes before the witching hour of midnight which can never be reached.

An interesting note about Marsaxlokk Bay is that Cold War history was made here in December 1989, when the Russian Soviet Leader Gorbachev and the American President

Bush Snr. met for two days of discussion on a moored warship. A terrible storm blew up while they were on board which gave a deal of damage to the flotilla and gave them both some discomfort. They must have been desperate to finalise a deal and to get back on to dry land. Despite the storm problems, an agreement was reached between them helping to bring an end to the Cold War conflict. Nicknamed 'The Seasick Summit', it is tempting to imagine that perhaps more discomfort in similar negotiations between leaders or politicians might also bring about speedy and successful conclusions.

At lunchtime, I walked along the quay past the daily market selling food, souvenirs and knick - knacks towards the celebrated fish restaurants, originally the fishermens' old family houses. Outside many of the restaurants a large variety of fresh fish were displayed on ice trays making dining at these establishment very attractive. I succumbed and enjoyed a delicious meal of sea bream.

I wanted to enter into conversation with some of the fishermen in order to be more informed about the life of a Maltese fisherman, but after many approaches and some monosyllabic replies, I discovered that the crews of the boats were either Egyptian or Indonesian. Eventually I managed to track down an old retired fisherman on the quay who told me that the Maltese youth are not interested in making fishing a career and that it is now impossible to crew a boat just with Maltese fishermen. The young want to study at school and better themselves.

I returned on the Sunday morning and as predicted there were large crowds of tourists milling around which made sketching in the market crush almost impossible. Despite the difficulties, I finally managed to make a few rough sketches and took some reference photographs so that I could complete the paintings back in the studio.

The dazzling array of different fish, shellfish, prawns, squid and octopus was fascinating, a window on the underwater world of the Mediterranean. The variety of fish included Lampuki - dolphin fish, Bazuga - sea bream, Spnotta - bass, Pixxispat - swordfish, Skorfnott - rock fish, Tonn - tuna, a large Cerna - grouper and Pagella - snapper fish.

I had, as it turned out, originally drawn a family of market traders and I was keen to get their reactions to my finished painting, so I returned on a Sunday afternoon when the family were starting to pack up their stall. Holding the painting up in front of them, I am pleased to say that I immediately got the surprised and delighted reaction I was hoping for. Other traders seeing the enthusiasm and interest my painting had engendered left their stalls and gathered round to have a look, eager to make their own comments. 'You painted this in

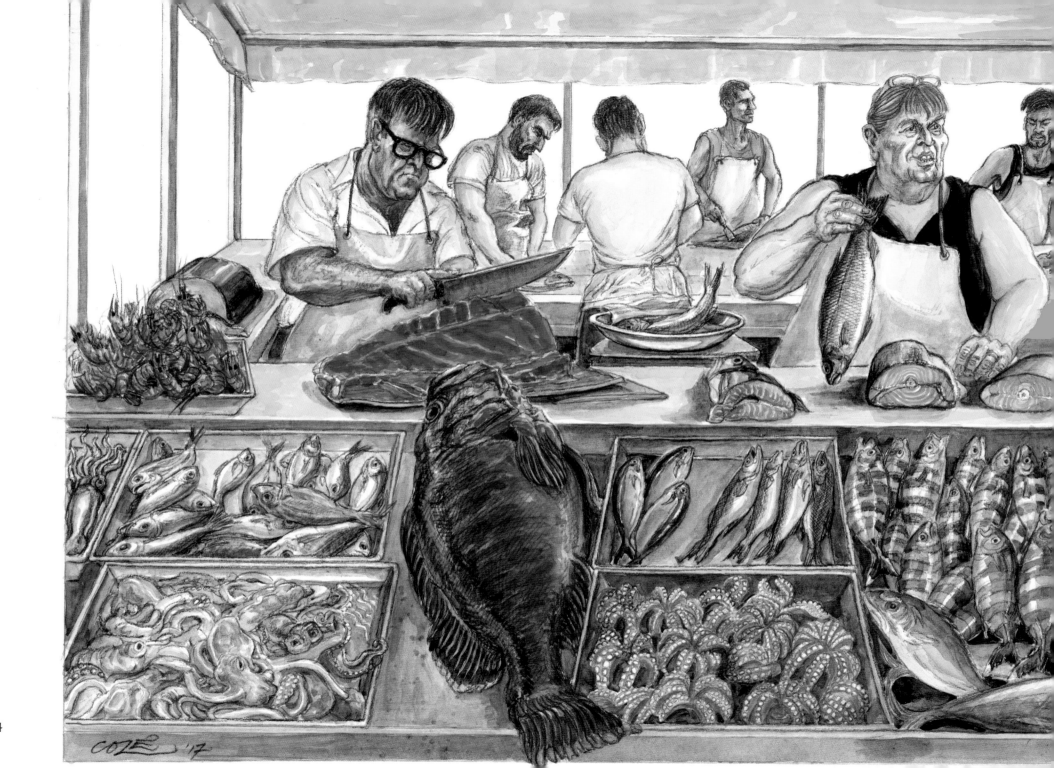

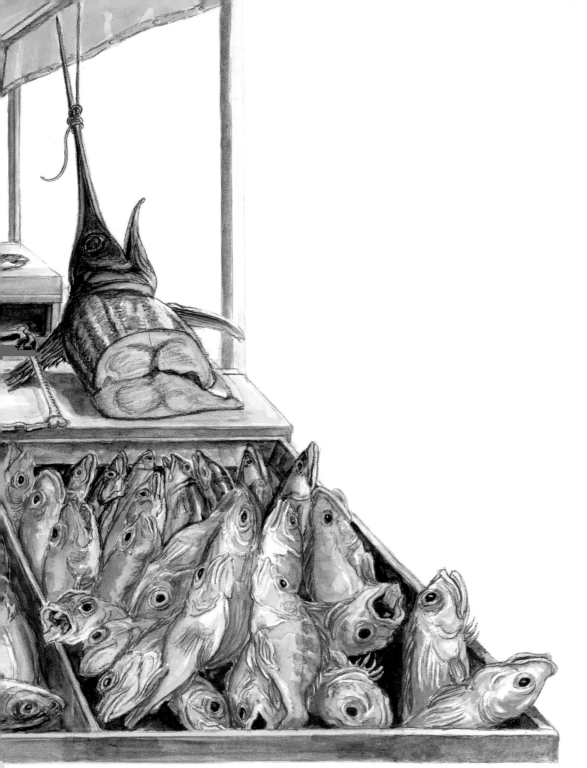

September, didn't you?' one asked. 'How do you know that?' I replied. 'Oh that's easy. You have painted pilot fish and they arrive in our waters that month.' I showed them the other paintings I had done in the harbour and got an amused reaction. 'Oh, that's my uncle's boat, fantastic!' 'You have drawn my father George Bugesh sorting his nets; he's 85, amazing!'

The family's name I was told was Maniscalco and they were from Marsaxlokk: father Michael, mother Vonney, sons John and Richard and nephew Azaki. Every Sunday morning with the exception of the last Sunday in July and the first in August during the Marsaxlokk Festival, they start work at 4am and begin setting up their stall with the fish bought from the market in Marsa. The eldest son John who now runs the business studied my painting closely. 'That's great, but I see that you have drawn me twice!' he declared, 'That's me, and that's my back.' He was right, I had. It took me by surprise, as I hadn't realised that I had inadvertently increased the size of their family by one. My justification of artistic licence drew little response. 'I did it in order to make a workable composition.' That at least was true. 'Two for the price of one!' John gave me a wry smile, but I could tell that he wasn't convinced.

HAGAR QIM AND MNAJDRA

The impressive Megalithic Temples of Hagar Qim and Mnajdra are situated on the southern edge of Malta on a steep hillside overlooking the sea. Hagar Qim is translated as standing stones and they comprise the first temple you enter after leaving the informative visitor centre.

On entering the temple's inner circle I discovered that there was a gap between the stones that framed a beautiful view of the tiny island of Filfla, which is uninhabited and a designated nature reserve. Unfortunately the island is peppered with unexploded shells thanks to the British navy who used it as target practice during the Second World War, but at least the bombs will have

the great advantage of protecting the wildlife by deterring unwelcome visitors.

Mnajdra Temple is sited lower down the coastal cliff and is older than Hagar Qim, dated between 3,600 - 3,000 BC. It consists of three temples, each of which is aligned differently in relation to the sun. When I first visited the two sites in 1975, they were both open to the elements and the impact was very dramatic on the coastal cliffs much as originally intended, but in order to protect them from further erosion, they are now both covered with a canopy.

The National Archaeological Museum in Valletta now houses most of the artefacts found on the sites, including the many female fertility figurines. Amongst these is the famous Maltese Venus with its enlarged sexual body parts. However, to my mind the most exciting and beautiful Megalithic statuette is the Sleeping Woman dated to 3600 - 2500 BC. It was found in the Hal Saflieni Hypogeum in Paola and is so extraordinarily modern in its concept that it could be happily exhibited alongside sculptures by Henry Moore.

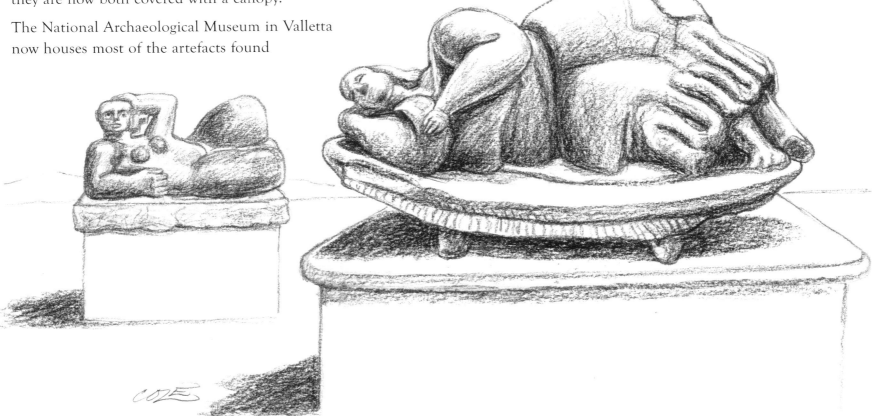

Paceville, the modern temple of lively night life, viewed from St Julian's showing the Portmaso Tower

The Blue Grotto, Wied iż - Żurrieq.

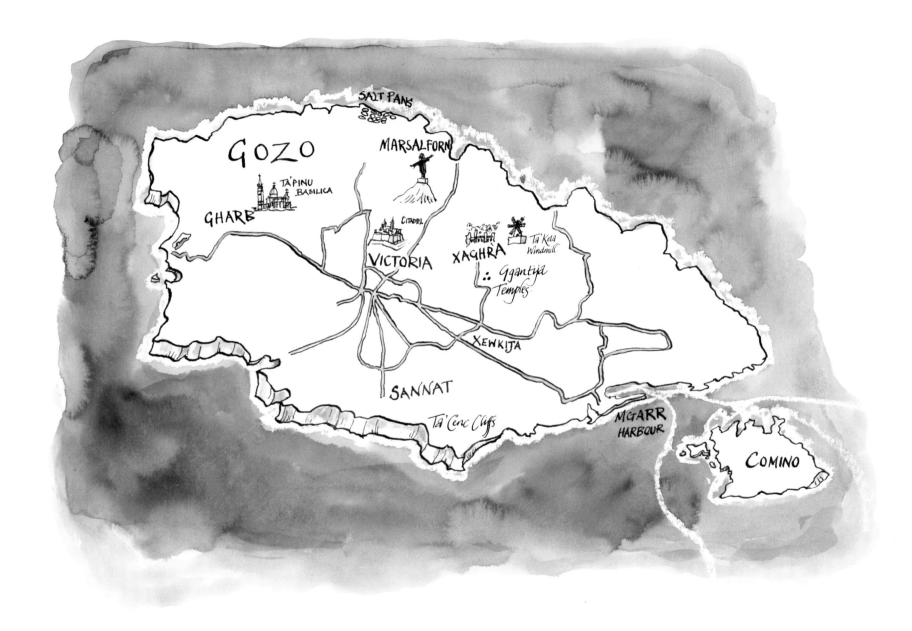

GOZO

AND COMINO

94

The facade of the Church drawn from the roof of the Courthouse

However, the Downtown Hotel where I first stayed is still active and the good news is that it has improved immeasurably over the years. Not all change is unwelcome.

View of The Citadel from the Bus Terminus. 101

TAS - SALVATUR HILL

One glorious sunny morning, I walked down the road from the Downtown Hotel in Victoria to explore the area. I discovered a lane with cacti skirting its edge that led me across the fields and opened up a beautiful distant view of a hill with a cross on its summit. This was Tas - Salvatur Hill. Wild flowers bloomed in abundance and I watched green lizards busy scurrying from rock to rock under the cacti hunting for food. The view was enchanting and I found a good spot to start sketching.

After about ten minutes I was aware of a roaring sound and three young cross - country motorcyclists suddenly appeared in the very narrow lane and rushed towards me. I hastily backed into the vegetation of prickly pears in fear of my life! Shaken but not stirred I gathered my thoughts, picked off the thorns and continued drawing with the scent of unwelcome exhaust fumes temporarily wafting around my nostrils.

The following day I set out to explore Tas - Salvatur Hill and took the bus to Marsalforn hoping that I would not meet any more unexpected cross - country track bikes. When we arrived on the outskirts of the town I could see the cross perched up high on the hill, but what I originally thought was a cross appeared to be a black sculpture of a Risen Christ with arms outstretched.

'The Lace Makers'. Watercolour and Crayon.

INDEPENDENCE SQUARE

I returned to Independence Square in Victoria clutching my original sketch from 1975, intent on doing an updated version. Carefully positioning myself as before when I had observed the priest and the nuns going about their daily work, I started drawing what I thought was the Church of St James the Greater at the end of the square. I immediately realised

that something was wrong. The church was different. I was puzzled; had I got lost and was now standing in the wrong square? I couldn't work it out, so I asked around the locals and got a number of confused replies. Finally I met a man who told me what had happened. Apparently the original church wanted to expand and so it was decided to build a basement room, but unfortunately, during construction of the cellar in 1979, the church collapsed into the excavation hole and was destroyed. A replacement church was constructed, so I had been drawing an entirely different building.

CARNIVAL

Over one February weekend every year, the islands of Malta come alive with Carnival. People of all ages dress up in a variety of colourful costumes and parade through the towns, performing and dancing their way to the main squares. Their themes usually involve animals, birds and insects, but there are also giant models of mythical characters.

These spectacular constructions are mainly built around tractors that are incorporated into the design and often cause surprise to passers - by as they move from town to town. They are technically sophisticated with many moving parts and, in Independence Square, I watched them transform into different shapes during the performances. One eye - catching structure featured maidens dancing on the deck of a boat among a giant's arms and surrounding sea horses. There was a great sense of enjoyment and audience participation as the dance troupes performed their routines to loud music with the grotesque, florescent - painted female sculptures being wheeled around.

Carnival Performance in Independence Square, Victoria.

115

St George's Square

St George's Square is situated behind Independence Square in the centre of Victoria. St George is an important figure in Gozo history as he is regarded as the protector of the island and his

liturgical feast is celebrated each year in the Basilica on the 23rd April, as it is in England where St George is also a patron saint. Interestingly, the colourful processions and festivities associated with St George don't appear in the city streets until the third Sunday in July.

The square in front of the Basilica attracts lots of tourists in the summer, happily eating outside at the restaurant and café tables arranged around its perimeter. Leading off the square are old, narrow maze - like streets and alleyways and many of the houses are decorated with traditional small statues of St George. At one street corner, I came across a large, unconventional sculpture of St George, primitive and naive. The figure was static, of indeterminate gender and age, to my mind at least; even the dragon seemed strangely relaxed and passive about the spear stuck in its gullet. I have seen some fantastic sculptures in Malta but this one was certainly odd. I do have to confess though, that the satirist in me did find it amusing and it was fun to draw.

However, the baroque Basilica of St George built between 1672 and 1678 does impress me. It was built in the shape of a Latin cross and has a total of 11 side chapels all heavily decorated. The Basilica justly gets its reputation as 'the golden church' of Gozo as it is covered entirely with marble and gold stucco. The entrance is through two impressively large modern bronze doors that are decorated with eight sculpted panels.

Additionally, the Basilica contains two outstanding works of art of St George: an altarpiece painting by Mattia Preti showing St George triumphant over the dragon and a wooden sculpture of the patron saint by Pietru Pawl Azzopardi.

Opera

You can imagine my surprise when walking along Republic Street in Victoria to find two opera houses on opposite sides of the street, and both still functioning. The fact that a small island the size of Gozo with a population of just 30,000 people can sustain and support one opera house would be remarkable, but two? That's astonishing.

These two local theatres, the Teatru Astra and the Teatru tal - Opera Aurora, have inspired and nurtured many famous performers in the international opera world, including two outstanding singers, the tenor Joseph Calleja and the soprano Miriam Cauchi.

Calleja was born at nearby Attard and made his debut at the Astra in 1997 as Macduff in Verdi's Macbeth at just 19 years old, and is now one of the most sought - after tenors for opera companies around the world. Cauchi also made her debut at the Astra theatre and performed the role of Oscar in Verdi's 'Un Ballo in Maschera' in 2002. She has become an important ambassador for Maltese vocal music and has recently recorded 'Art songs from Malta' by Vella. She was awarded the National Order of Merit by the President of Malta.

Opera has often been regarded as entertainment only attended by and enjoyed by the establishment classes, but here it is available to all Gozitans. They have always had a love of religious pageants, musical entertainment and theatrical productions and a long history of producing events. Recognising this musical evolution are two well - crafted

sculptures on the facade of the Aurora Opera house, dedicated to two early pioneers of musical development in Gozo, the conductor Dirjanu Lanzon and Gorg Tabone.

The story behind the Aurora theatre sculptures is one of national pride. In order to honour their patron saint, Saint Margaret, Virgin and Martyr, the village of Ta Sannat had been entertained since 1813 at their traditional festa by a band. The big problem was that the musicians were all Maltese rather than Gozitan. This caused resentment among the proud patriotic locals,

DIRJANU LANZON
1820 - 1894

but thanks to the energy and drive of Dirjanu Lanzon and Gorg Tabone during the middle of the 19th century, a group of Gozitan musicians was brought together and, in 1846, the

Leone Brass Band was formed to play at the festa. Their influence continues today.

The Astra theatre has the reputation of being one of the oldest functioning theatres in the world and is more traditional in its choice of icons on its façade, displaying portrait busts of the classical composers, Beethoven, Verdi and one I sadly don't recognise for sure, but is probably Mozart.

As you can imagine, the rivalry between the two theatres is a passionate affair and every year the people of the Aurora Opera House (with its Leone

GORG TABONE
1841 - 1916

Philharmonic Society) and those of the Astra Theatre (with its La Stella Philharmonic Society) compete to put on the finest and best opera production. It is the high quality of their performances often with international soloists that has brought them a great following among opera enthusiasts. Both theatres rely on enthusiastic volunteers to stage the productions with a mix of amateur and professional singers and musicians, and they work hard to generate audiences and funding to sustain the tradition of presenting at least one major opera production annually. It's a big task, but has put Gozo on the international opera map.

In 2017, the Aurora Opera Company commemorated their 40th anniversary since their first opera performance - Puccini's Madame Butterfly in 1977. They celebrated with a new production of the opera in April, followed in October by a double bill on the same evening of Mascagni's Cavalleria Rusticana and Leoncavallo's Pagliacci.

Not to be outdone, in 2018 the Teatru Astra celebrated the 50th anniversary of its incorporation with the Soċjetà Filarmonika La Stella, a musical society founded in 1863, with a production of Verdi's La Traviata. This collaboration has proved to be a fruitful relationship, and over the recent decades the theatre has staged many high quality musicals such as Grease and Evita, and a wide variety of other shows. Top - class singers and performers direct from the best theatres, opera houses and concert halls around the world have featured in a wide - ranging programme.

Unfortunately the theatre was badly damaged by an extensive electrical fire in 2003, and has had to be refurbished in the subsequent two years. Happily the theatre

can now boast an acoustically perfect auditorium making it the best of its kind on the Maltese islands.

The facades of the two opera houses are very different, but their entrance foyers are gloomily similar with huge dark interiors; they function as popular bars, cafés and snooker halls keeping the theatres alive when there are no other performances. I looked in one evening in February when I was passing and was surprised to find that the foyers of not one but both theatres were full to bursting with elderly citizens playing bingo. Of course, opera can't be sustained throughout the whole year, but there are a great variety of other entertainments for people to enjoy.

View of the church of St John the Baptist, Xewkija.

Eroded sculptures of saints placed outside the Church of St Margaret in Sannat.

TA' KOLA WINDMILL

The windmill is situated at the entrance to the village of Xaghra. The Ggantija Prehistoric Temples are but a stone's throw away. The name Ta' Kola is derived from the nickname of the miller Zeppu ta' Kola who blew a triton - shell to inform the local farmers that he was ready to grind their corn. Rebuilt in the 1780s it is one of the last surviving windmills on the islands and has been recently restored. It no longer operates as a mill but as a folklore and traditional tool museum.

THE LAST MILLER

Guzeppi Grech was born in Xaghra to a family of millers in 1900 and lived to the good old age of 87, travelling widely. He survived fighting in the bitter Gallipoli Campaign during the First World War when, in 1915, the Allied soldiers (with many from Australia and New Zealand) suffered a horrendous defeat against the Ottoman forces. Returning to Gozo for four years, he migrated to Australia and worked in the sugar cane fields and then in a hazardous lead factory. When his father died six years later, he returned to Gozo and although working for a short period in Tunisia, he eventually took over the running of the family Ta' Kola windmill.

Grech had developed great expertise and knowledge as a millwright and he was able to repair old abandoned windmills needed during the Second World War as fuel for the steam - driven mills ran out. He was tall and well built, with fair hair, a ruddy complexion and a reputation for hard work, and despite being illiterate he was master of all trades. To my mind he lived an extraordinary varied life.

There is a large collection of his own tools displayed in the museum that illustrate his undoubted skills and versatility.

COMINO

I have viewed the island of Comino many times whilst sailing on the ferry from Malta to Gozo. It seemed to have an intriguing almost desolate air about it. The only visible human landmark seen from the sea is the fortified St Mary's Watchtower, sitting high on the cliffs. The watchtower was built by the Grand Master Alof de Wignacourt in 1618 to protect the few inhabitants on Comino from pirate attacks. Nowadays, the island is populated by a few resident families and there is a hotel for tourists.

In 2018 I finally made the trip to the island on a small ferry from the harbour in Mġarr and was not disappointed. It is certainly a very beautiful island with the famous crystal clear waters of the Blue Lagoon perfect for swimming and snorkelling. The landing stage on the island is now busy with boats of all sizes ferrying in tourists and the area is built up with caravans dispensing fast food and drinks. I was surprised to see that there was even a left luggage stand set up by an entrepreneur.

However, when you move away from the tourist hot spots along the cliffs towards the watchtower, the peace and tranquillity of the deserted island takes you over. I was seated on a rock sketching the bathers in the Blue Lagoon when a young man behind me shouted out 'Careful sir, there is a poisonous snake in the shrub behind you!' I didn't question his authority on poisonous snakes at the time, but I very cautiously turned round not wishing to frighten it into an attacking pose. It was, I discovered to my relief, not poisonous but a large brown lizard inches away from my backside with its head rooting for insects in the soil. For the record it turned out

to be an ocellated skink. Obviously a friendly inhabitant! The ocellated skink hidden in the shrubbery behind me was not enormous, about 8ins in length although I am told they can grow up to 12ins. Interestingly, although they have tiny legs these are not much good in an emergency; when attacked by a

predator it tucks them in and slithers away like a snake. It wasn't the only friendly creature I was to come across as I could hear in the distance the familiar but very surprising and unexpected cry of a peacock. My curiosity stirred, I started out on a circular tour along the coast searching for the bird. Passing by St Mary's Watchtower I came across a complex of run - down deserted buildings that had once been a 19th century isolation hospital, built by the British military authorities to house troops returning to Malta from plague - stricken Middle Eastern ports. Then the cry of the peacock suddenly burst out, and there it was

in all its feathered glory roosting on top of a building. Comino has become a bird sanctuary protecting the yelkonan sheerwater nesting on the steep cliffs where there are around 80 - 140 pairs. Sadly they are threatened not only by indigenous rats, but inevitably human recreational activity.

Comino had once been, following the French occupation of Malta, a place of exile and imprisonment for criminals and pro - French sympathisers. Nowadays I think it would be a wonderful island to be exiled on. It has beautiful coves, rock formations, exotic flora and fauna, the unexpected reptile and bird life, and above all, peace and tranquillity.

The Ocellated Skink

Xwejni Salt Pans

Walking westward along the sea coast from Marsalforn, you discover the salt pans of Xwejni that stretch for about three kilometres in front of a dramatic and colourful section of eroded cliffs.

The production of salt is a long established tradition dating back some 350 years to Phoenician and Roman times, and sustained by dedicated Gozitan families. The pans are cut out from the rock in grid - like patterns and filled with water pumped from the sea. The water evaporates in the hot summer sun and a film of salt is then harvested. Most of the strenuous work is done very early in the morning to escape the intense heat of the summer months and the salt is swept into glistening mounds. Once gathered up, the salt is stored in caves that have been carved out of the cliffs, packaged up, and then offered for sale to the public.

Comino viewed from a path above the wild cliffs of Ta'Cenc.

ACKNOWLEDGEMENTS

I would like to thank all those whose valuable contributions made this book possible.

My ever - supportive wife Felicity, who has tolerated with fortitude my love of Malta and who encouraged the production of this book.

Robin Cannon, the designer of the pages, for his infinite patience in dealing with me.

Alan Giddings, who willingly took on the challenging task of editing my text.

Mary and Derek Nice, the family of Victor Pasmore, who gave me a valuable insight into his work and experience of the island.

Michael Lowell for his wealth of knowledge of Malta and its traditions, and the support that he generously offered me towards the book's publication.

Joe Borg for his help and guidance in the publication of the book.

Marika Azzopardi with whom I discussed my original concept for the book.

I am grateful to those who have given me permission to reproduce my original paintings and drawings from their collections.

Shrine of 'Souls in Pergatory' on the road to Sannat

BIOGRAPHY

Richard Cole was born in 1942, and studied painting at Wimbledon School of Art.

After graduating, he taught for five years and then carved out a career as a caricaturist, political cartoonist and reportage artist.

He contributed regularly to *The Daily Express*, *The Times*, *The Sunday Times*, *The Sunday* and *Daily Telegraph*, *The Guardian*, and worked as the European contract artist for American television's *CBS News*.

He has drawn major political debates in *The House of Commons* and terrorist trials in Europe, and was in Lyon for the trial in 1991 of the notorious Nazi war criminal,

Klaus Barbie. His drawings were published in *The Observer* newspaper.

In 2004, Cole was the sole court artist in Baghdad for the courts - martial of American soldiers accused of torture at the *Abu Ghraib Prison* in Iraq.

He has exhibited his work in British and French galleries, and now divides his time between his studios in France and the United Kingdom.

WORK IN PUBLIC COLLECTIONS

The British Museum, The Bank of England Museum, Wimbledon Tennis Museum, Samlung Karikaturen and The Cartoon Museum, Basel, Switzerland, The Ashmolean Museum Oxford.

www.richardcoleltd.com

Boat maintenance in Marsaxlokk harbour.